MY FIRST BODY BOOK
Head to Toes

Zita Newcome

WALKER BOOKS

AND SUBSIDIARIES

LONDON · BOSTON · SYDNEY · AUCKLAND

Contents

Bodies

Our bodies are made up of lots of different parts.
How many can you name?

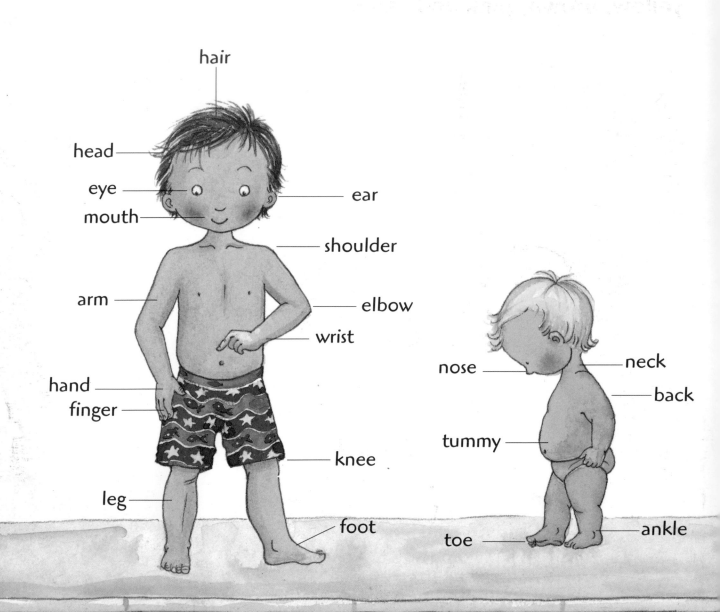

hair

head

eye

mouth

ear

shoulder

arm

elbow

wrist

hand

finger

knee

leg

foot

nose

neck

back

tummy

toe

ankle

Bodies come in different shapes and sizes.
Some are small, some are tall, some are fat, some are thin.
They are covered in skin which can be all sorts of colours ...
yellow, brown, pink and black.

Faces

Faces tell us a lot about people and how they are feeling.

happy

sad

cheeky

shy

surprised

sleepy

frightened

snooty

angry

grumpy

Eyes

We use our eyes for seeing with.
Do you know what colour yours are?
Are they brown or green, blue or grey?

8

Some people wear glasses to help them see better and some people wear dark glasses to protect their eyes from the sun. When we are upset we cry, and tears come from our eyes.

Noses

We use our noses for smelling with, and breathing through.
Think of smells you like ... and ones you don't like.

Mouths

We use our mouths for eating and drinking. We taste food with our tongues and bite and chew it with our teeth.
How many teeth do you have?

sing   make faces   kiss   gasp   lick

Think of all the other things you can do with your mouth.

smile   laugh   blow bubbles   stick your tongue out   shush   yell

Ears

We use our ears for hearing with. Listen carefully.
How many noises can you hear? Are they loud or quiet?
Some noises are nice … and some are not so nice.

Hair

Hair keeps our head warm and protects it from the sun. People have different kinds of hair.

straight

messy

short

curly

long

We need to care for our hair to keep it healthy. Hair needs:

washing

brushing and combing

cutting

We can also have fun with hair. 17

Arms and Hands

We use our arms and hands
to pick things up and hold things.
Look at what else we can do
with them.

handstand

paint

wave

clap

count

build

mix   roll   squeeze   press

stroke

hold hands

shake

push

Legs and Feet

We use our legs and feet
to stand and walk.
Look at what else we
can do with them.

dance

crouch   kick   run

stand on one leg   tiptoe   twist   tap-dance   stamp

jump   pedal   splash   paddle

Look Inside!

Our bodies are held up by a bony frame called a skeleton. If we didn't have a skeleton we would be as wobbly as jelly! There are lots of different bones in a skeleton. Which can you feel through your skin?

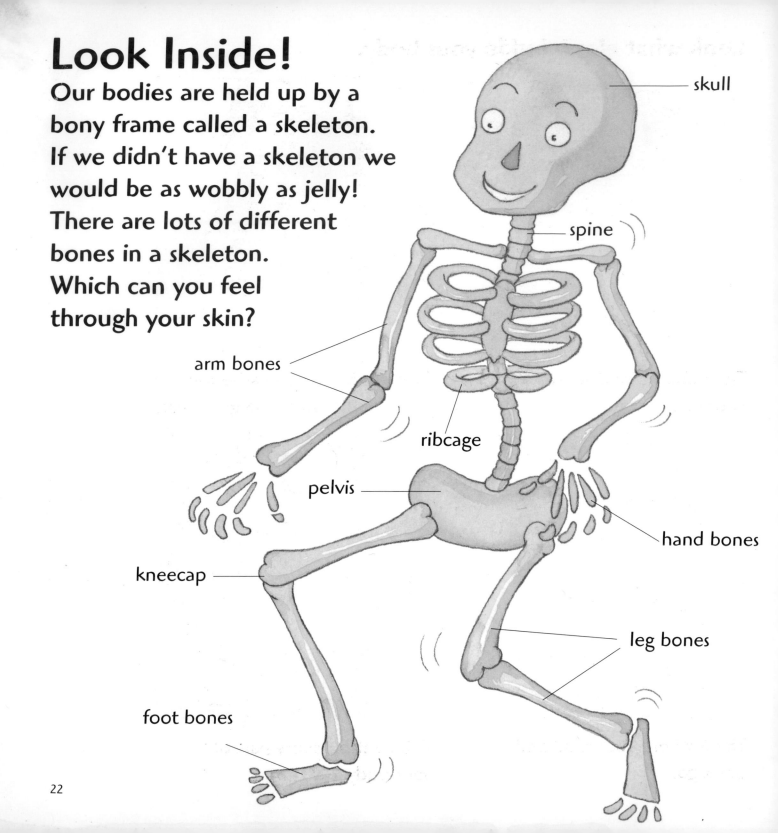

skull

spine

arm bones

ribcage

pelvis

hand bones

kneecap

leg bones

foot bones

Look what else is inside your body.

heart

lungs

This pumps blood round
your body.

The air that you breathe through
your mouth and nose goes here.

stomach

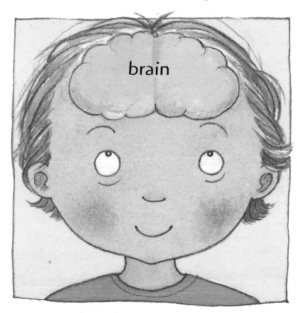

brain

This is where your food and
drink go.

This controls every part of
your body.

Body Care

We need to look after our bodies to keep ourselves well and happy. We need to eat and drink each day to give them energy. We need to sleep to give them a rest. We need to keep them clean. And we need to make sure they aren't too hot or too cold.

What would you wear if it was cold?
What would you wear if it was hot?
What would you wear if it was raining?

Hurt and Unwell Bodies

All our bodies hurt or feel unwell sometimes.
They take a little while to get better.

Which of these has been wrong with your body?

runny nose

tummy-ache

cut

sprain

bruise

splinter

chickenpox

temperature

earache

When You Were a Baby...

When you were born you were a tiny baby like this. Every day you grew bigger ... and bigger ... and bigger... As the weeks passed, you learned how to do more and more.

| lie | roll | push up | sit | crawl |

play peepo   talk   feed yourself

stand   wobble   take steps   walk   run

What Can You Do Now?

Now you can do lots of things with your body.
Which of these can you do?

climb upstairs

draw a picture

catch a ball

do up buttons

get dressed

brush your teeth

use the toilet

hop

put on your shoes

jump in the water

ride a bicycle

sing a song   play the recorder

open the door

brush your hair

read a book

For Rebecca and Elizabeth

First published 2000 by Walker Books Ltd
87 Vauxhall Walk, London SE11 5HJ

This edition published 2009

2 4 6 8 10 9 7 5 3 1

The right of Zita Newcome to be identified as author/illustrator of this work has been asserted
by her in accordance with the Copyright, Designs and Patents Act 1988

This book has been typeset in ITC Highlander

Printed in China

British Library Cataloguing in Publication Data:
a catalogue record for this book is available from the British Library

ISBN 978-1-4063-2225-5

www.walker.co.uk